Spark!

words and pictures for activating English

WORKBOOK 1

Name:

Class:

Address:

Phone:

Beth Haynes

ACTUAL

First published 2004
Second edition 2006
Printed in Australia by Southwood Press

Acknowledgements
While every care has been taken to trace and acknowledge copyright, the publishers tender their apologies for any accidental infringement.

ISBN 0-9750208-5-4

ACTUAL

Actual Enterprises
PO Box 14 Glebe 2037
spark@actual.com.au
www.actual.com.au

Note for Teachers:

How Spark! Works

The English language is rich and complex, and can be overwhelming. The ***Spark!*** series provides your students with clear signposting and pathways.

Spark! offers a solid foundation of comprehensible input for teachers to build upon. The pictures, words, and grammatical patterns have been carefully selected to clarify and develop basic language skills in meaningful contexts.

Our aim is to fully engage students, to activate all areas, and to bring in all the processing strategies. This calls for a balance and movement between:

- topics and skills
- spoken and written language
- cooperative and independent tasks
- structure and risk-taking
- personal/specific and general
- everyday and school-based work

We also want to make learning purposeful and enjoyable – so that all students can succeed at whichever level they are working towards.

The teacher is the vital link in bringing these textbooks and language to life. With teacher scaffolding, the students can go further.

Here are some general guidelines

Get to know the Wordbank

First, show the students how to navigate the ***Wordbank***. For example, let them find topics, talk about what they like and what they did, and colour the colours. The ***Wordbank*** is a resource which links in with the ***Workbook*** activities, and which students will also refer to at other times.

Present the Workbook task

You will want to present the vocabulary, topics and activities of the ***Workbooks*** according to your own teaching strategies and the needs of your students. Brainstorm existing knowledge, use the board and overhead transparencies, 'go through' the work with them, practise pronunciation, personalise, contextualise and motivate.

As an example, first model the language and requirements of communicative activities with the whole class. Also, concepts such as syllables (pages 48-50) will need simple explanation.

Do the task

When students are clear about the what, how and why of tasks, they will be able to carry them out in a focussed way.

Follow-up and extend

After that, the teacher can provide follow-up, consolidation and extension. If your students are weaker, they may need more unpacking and scaffolding, and fewer items. For stronger students, more challenging, open-ended work can be incorporated.

You can devise any spin-off activities you like – such as flashcards, jazz chants, bingo, change chairs game – as well as connecting the work in ***Spark!*** with further lessons.

Sounds & Spelling Reference

Note that with the *Sounds and Spelling Reference,* the intention is not to be exhaustive. It is to provide an overview while clarifying many of the complexities within the system. Students will learn little by little, by a steady process of approximation.

As teachers, we have the opportunity to channel students' drive to access, structure and communicate meanings in language; to engage with new knowledge and values; to develop emotionally, socially and creatively; and to gain confidence through success.

Contents

Choose the Word (1)

Put a circle around the correct word in each row.

1.		*plate*	*plane*	*play*	*paint*
2.		*cat*	*cap*	*card*	*take*
3.		*son*	*soon*	*seen*	*sun*
4.		*kite*	*cat*	*take*	*talk*
5.		*a*	*eye*	*I*	*air*
6.		*clock*	*cook*	*kick*	*cake*
7.		*paper*	*apple*	*people*	*purple*
8.		*potato*	*foot*	*photo*	*hot*
9.	10	*ten*	*net*	*tan*	*then*
10.		*thing*	*sink*	*sing*	*zing*

The Alphabet (1)

Copy the letters of the alphabet in small letters.

a	n
b	o
c	p
d	q
e	r
f	s
g	t
h	u
i	v
j	w
k	x
l	y
m	z

The Alphabet (2)

Copy the letters of the alphabet in CAPITAL LETTERS.

A N
B O
C P
D Q
E R
F S
G T
H U
I V
J W
K X
L Y
M Z

Same Letters

Which letter is the same?

Circle the same letter.

1.	a	g	d	(a)	c
2.	p	b	d	q	p
3.	i	j	i	l	t
4.	m	h	n	w	m
5.	u	u	n	v	w
6.	b	p	b	d	g
7.	g	a	q	p	g
8.	r	h	n	r	i
9.	v	n	w	v	u
10.	w	w	u	m	n

Same Words (1)

Which word is the same?

Match the words in CAPITAL LETTERS with the words in small letters.
Then copy the words next to each other in your own way.

TREE	hi	THREE	ok
GOOD	no	ME	bad
HI	who	YOU	how
YES	tree	OK	you
WHO	good	ON	three
NO	bye	BAD	off
OF	yes	HOW	me
BYE	of	OFF	on

TREE tree

What are they? (1)A

What is it? What's this?

Write the names under the pictures.
(You can find them in 'Spark! Wordbank.')

house	pencil	stamp	tomato
flower	TV	mouth	bike
photo	flag	park	

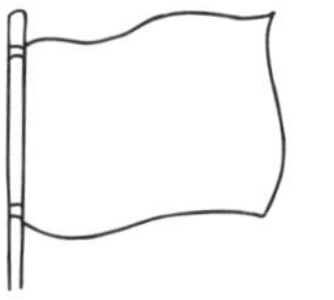

What are they? (1)B

What is this? Make sentences.

FULL STOP

▸ This is a __________.

1. This is a park.

2.

3.

4.

5.

6.

7.

8.

9.

10.

11.

Numbers

Copy the numerals.

0	
1	11
2	12
3	13
4	14
5	15
6	16
7	17
8	18
9	19
10	20
	100
	1000

Numbers & Words (1)

Write the number words in numerals.

zero 0	
one	eleven
two	twelve
three	thirteen
four	fourteen
five	fifteen
six	sixteen
seven	seventeen
eight	eighteen
nine	nineteen
ten	twenty

Numbers & Words (2)

Write the numbers in words.

0 zero	
1	11
2	12
3	13
4	14
5	15
6	16
7	17
8	18
9	19
10	20

➡ Talking and Listening:

Numbers & Words(3)A

Student A:

Tell your numbers to your partner – Student B on the next page. (DON'T LOOK at the next page.)
Write the numbers your partner tells you.
Then write the words. Then change and be Student B.

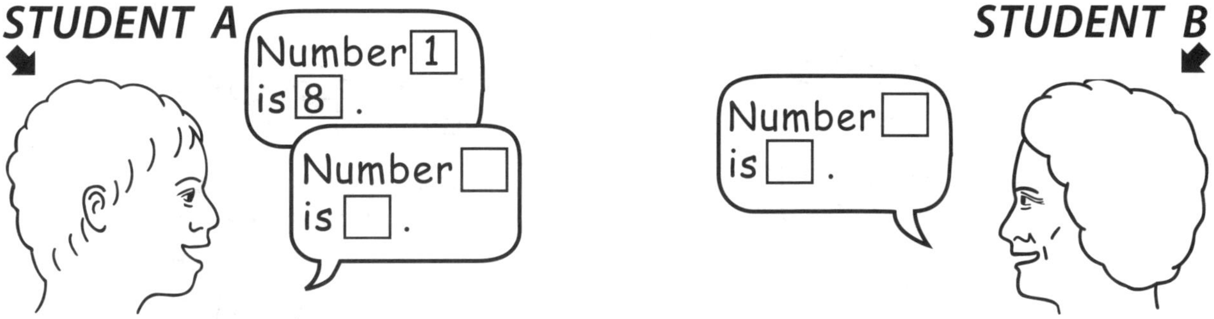

1. 8 eight
2.
3. 3
4.
5. 20
6.
7. 17
8.
9. 1
10.
11. 19
12.
13. 18
14.
15. 2
16.
17. 9
18.
19. 10
20.

➡ Talking and Listening: 

Numbers & Words(3)B

Student B:

Tell your numbers to your partner – Student A on the last page. (DON'T LOOK at the last page.)
Write the numbers your partner tells you.
Then write the words. Then change and be Student A.

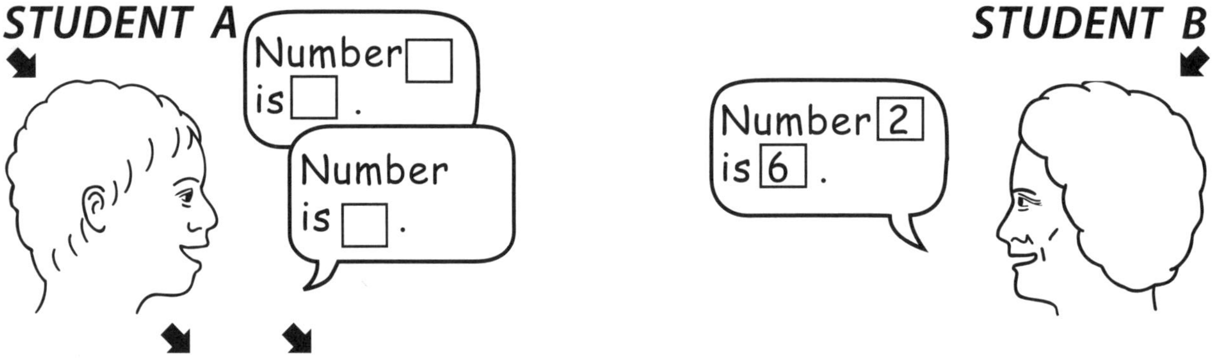

1. 8	11.
➡ 2. 6 six	12. 4
3.	13.
4. 13	14. 5
5.	15.
6. 12	16. 14
7.	17.
8. 7	18. 16
9.	19.
10. 11	20. 15

One to Ten

Copy these number words into the correct word shapes.
Also write the numerals.

seven	ten	three
two	one	five
six	eight	nine
four		

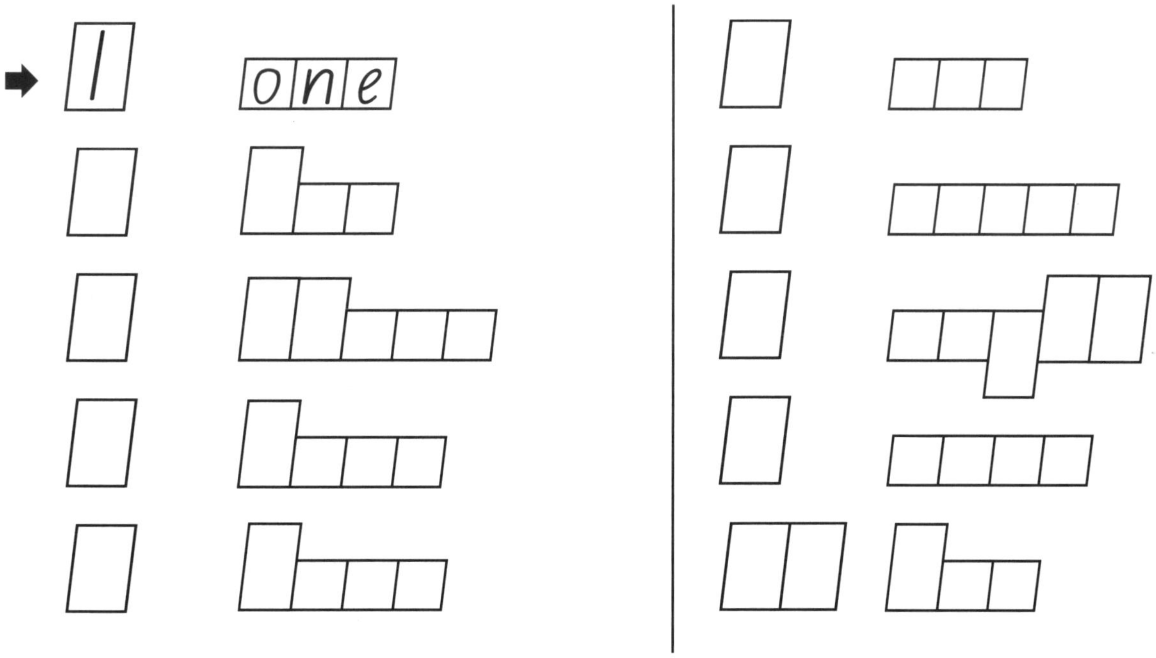

Eleven to Twenty

Copy these number words into the correct word shapes.
Also write the numerals.

sixteen	eleven	eighteen
thirteen	nineteen	twelve
seventeen	twenty	fifteen
fourteen		

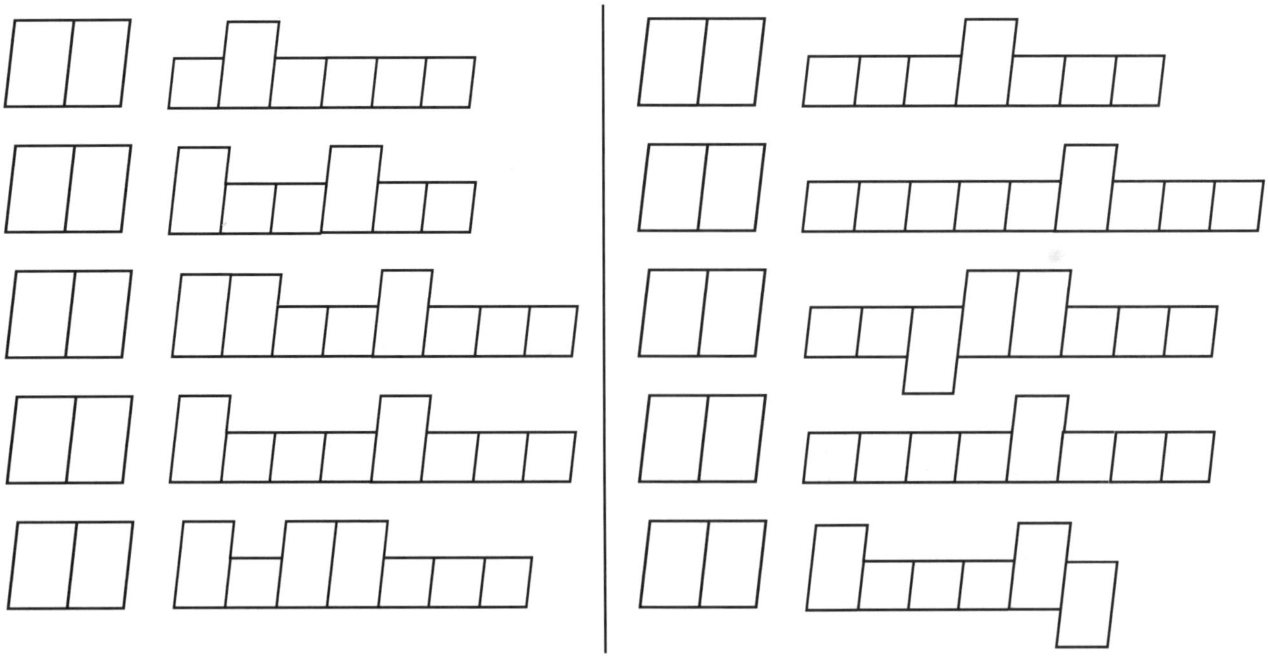

➡ Talking and Listening:

Hi!

Talking with a friend:

Write the missing words in this conversation. Then read the conversation with your classmate.

you go Goodbye	eating Hi about	are Where I'm	See What I've	going shops Good	listening And

What are they? (2)A

What is it? What's this?

Write the names under the pictures of the nouns.

cake	cap	drum	street
baby	shirt	bird	train
city	beach	computer	

What are they? (2)B

What is this? Make sentences.

FULL STOP

▶ This is a ________.

1. This

2.

3.

4.

5.

6.

7.

8.

9.

10.

11.

How many? (1)

How many are there?

- **How many** cats **are there?**
- **There are** 9 cats.

1. There are  9 Cats.
2. There are  7 boocks.
3. There are 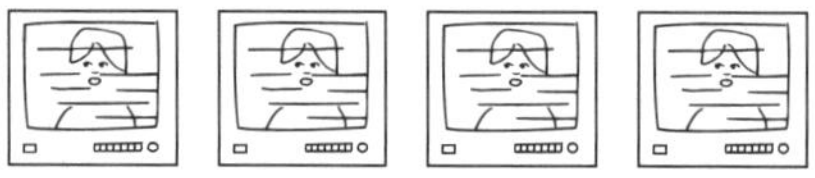 4 TV.
4. There are  12 Eggs.
5. There are  8 Rings.
6. There are  6 bye Biks.
7. There are  11 stars.
8. There are  5 Mini Markets.

9. There are  3 Childrens.
10. There are  15 Rounds.
11. There are  ☐ ________.
12. There are  ☐ Hands.

How many? (2)A

Student A:

Ask and tell your partner. Write the answers.

STUDENT A **STUDENT B**

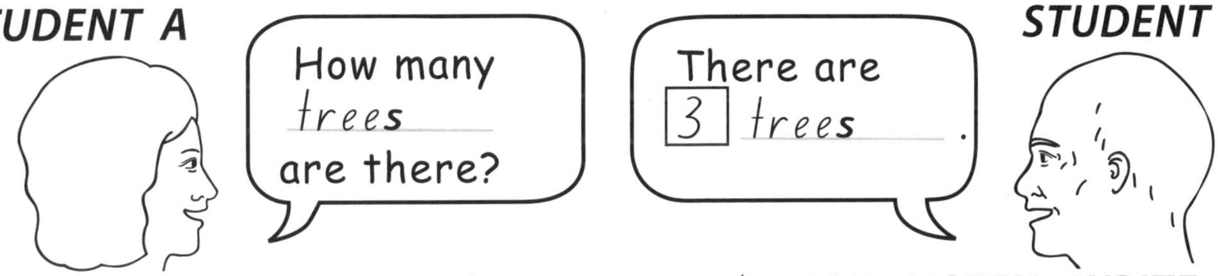

1. How many trees are there? ⬅ **ASK, LISTEN, WRITE.**

   There are ☐ ________.

2. How many ball are there? ⬅ **LISTEN, WRITE, TELL.**

   There are  ☐ ball.

3. How many hats are there?

   There are ☐ P________.

4. How many Pencil are there?

   There are  ☐ Pencils.

5. How many ducks are there?

   There are ☐ ________.

6. How many Apple are there?

   There are 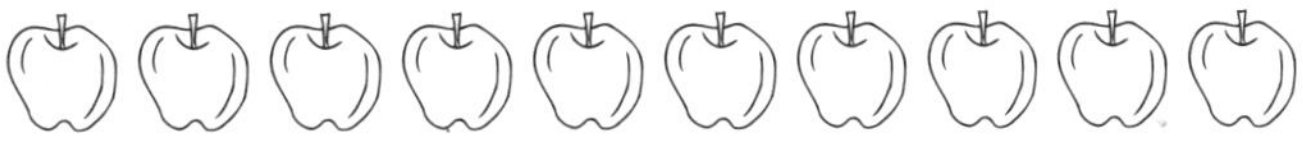 ☐ Apples.

7. How many cups are there?

   There are ☐ cups.

8. How many can are there?

   There are  ☐ can.

➡ Talking and Listening:

How many? (2)B

Student B:

Tell and ask your partner. Write the answers.

STUDENT A

How many trees are there?

There are [3] trees.

STUDENT B

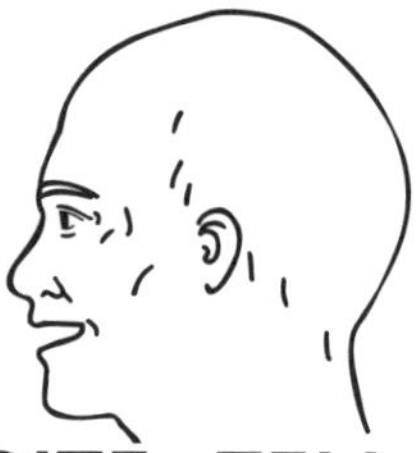

1. How many ________ are there? ⬅ **LISTEN, WRITE, TELL.**

   There are  [ ] ________.

2. How many balls are there? ⬅ **ASK, LISTEN, WRITE.**

   There are [4] balls.

3. How many hats are there?

   There are 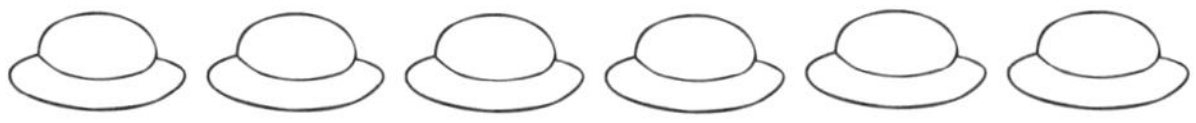 [6] hats.

4. How many pens are there?

   There are [3] Pencil.

5. How many dacks are there?

   There are  [7] dacks.

6. How many apples are there?

   There are [2] Apples.

7. How many ________ are there?

   There are  [ ] ________.

8. How many cars are there?

   There are [3] cars.

Same Words (2)

Which word is the same?

Circle the same word.

1.	stop	tops	pots	stop	post
2.	tell	let	feel	fell	tell
3.	who	what	how	won	who
4.	now	on	one	now	won
5.	good	cook	food	cool	good
6.	of	to	off	for	of
7.	walk	walk	make	talk	work
8.	letter	little	letter	feet	left
9.	table	apple	little	battle	table
10.	go	got	go	ago	do
11.	word	walk	work	word	world
12.	name	name	mane	mean	rain
13.	thought	through	taught	though	thought
14.	left	felt	tell	left	flat

Alphabet Puzzle (1)

What are they called?

What is it called?
Find the names in 'Spark! Wordbank'.
Then write the names under the pictures.
There is one noun for each letter of the alphabet.

1. ______________

2. ______________

3. ______________

4. ______________

5. ______________

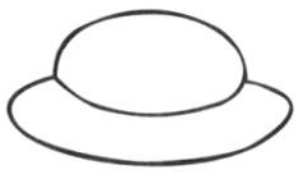
6. ______________

7. ______________

8. ______________

9. ______________

10. ______________

11. ______________

12. ______________

13. ______________

14. ______________

?
15. ______________

16. ______________

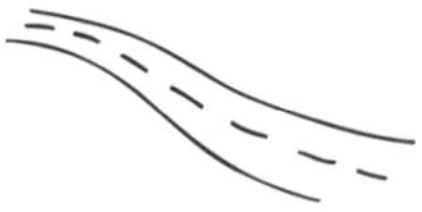
17. ______________

18. ______________

19. ______________

20. ______________

21. ______________

22. ______________

23. ______________

24. ______________

25. ______________

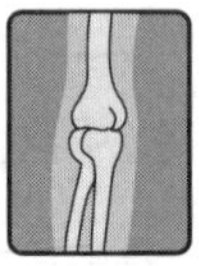
26. x-ray

Alphabet Puzzle (2)

Crossword Puzzle

Write the words onto the crossword puzzle.
They go ACROSS ➡ and DOWN ⬇.

Alphabet Puzzle (3)

Alphabetical Order

Write the words from the crossword puzzle – from the last 2 pages – in alphabetical order.

a	apple	j		s	
b		k		t	
c		l		u	
d		m		v	
e		n		w	
f		o		x	
g		p		y	
h		q		z	
i		r			

Alphabet Puzzle (4)

What are these?

What is this? Use the words from the puzzle to make sentences (in alphabetical order).

▸ This is a / (an) apple ________.

A. This is an ________

B. This is a ________

C. ________

D. ________

E. ________ an ________

F. ________

G. ________

H. ________

I. ________ an ________

J. ________

K. ________

L. ________

M. ________

N. ________

O. ________ an ________

P. ________ some ________

Q. ________

R. ________

S. ________

T. ________

U. ________ an ________

V. These are ________

W. ________

X. ________ an ________

Y. ________

Z. ________

Sport (1)

What are these sports?

What is this sport?
Study the names in 'Spark! Wordbank'.
Then write the names under the pictures.

1. across

10.

11.

8.

3.

5.

4.

2.

7.

9.

6.

1. down

Sport (2)

Crossword Puzzle

Write the nouns onto the crossword puzzle.
They go ACROSS ➡ and DOWN ⬇.

➡ Talking and Listening:

Sport (3)

What sports do you like?

▶ *Do you like table tennis?*

Ask your classmates and tick ☑ or cross ☒.

	NAME							
1.	table tennis							
2.	soccer							
3.	volleyball							
4.	softball							
5.	tai chi							
6.	basketball							
7.	tennis							
8.	rugby							
9.	netball							
10.	gym							
11.	cricket							
12.	badminton							

Sport (4)

What sports do you like?

Write sentences about yourself and your classmates.

- *I like* basketball .
- *Lucas likes* soccer and volleyball .

1.
2.
3.
4.
5.
6.
7.
8.
9.
10.
11.
12.
13.
14.
15.
16.

Making Words (1)

One-Syllable Words A

Join the first letters with the endings to make rhyming words.

1. b, c, t, l, sh → ook

book

2. b, s, m, gl, d, h → ad

3. s, b, tr, thr, f, fr, kn → ee

4. m, l, n, r, br, f, fl, fr, s, t → ight

5. n, g, h, l, sh → ot

6. d, s, w, p, pl, m → ay

M

7. b, c, m, r, s, f, h → at

at

8. p, m, t, th, wh → en

Making Words (2)

One-Syllable Words B

Continue joining the first letters with the endings to make rhyming words.

9.

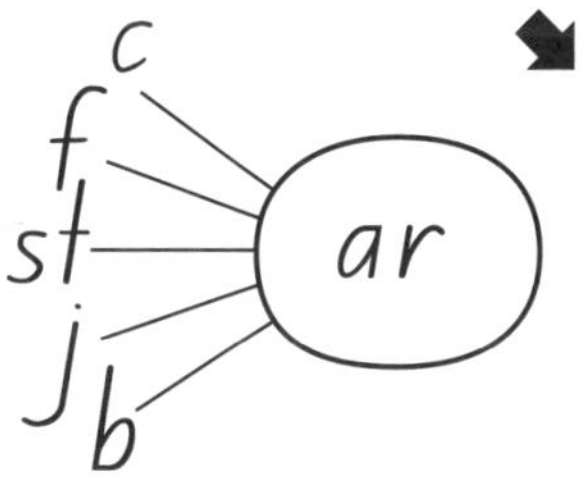

10.

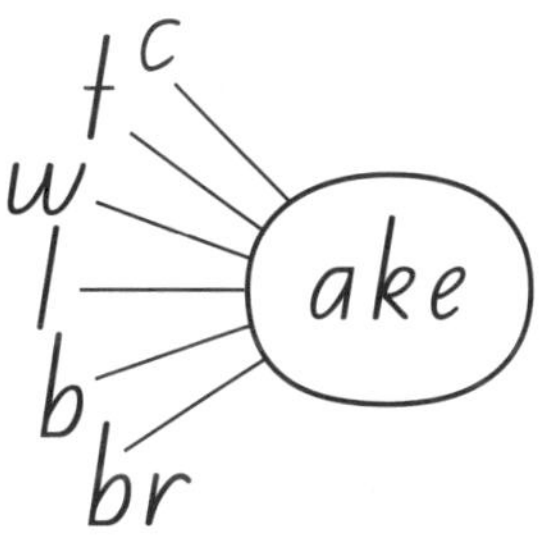

11.

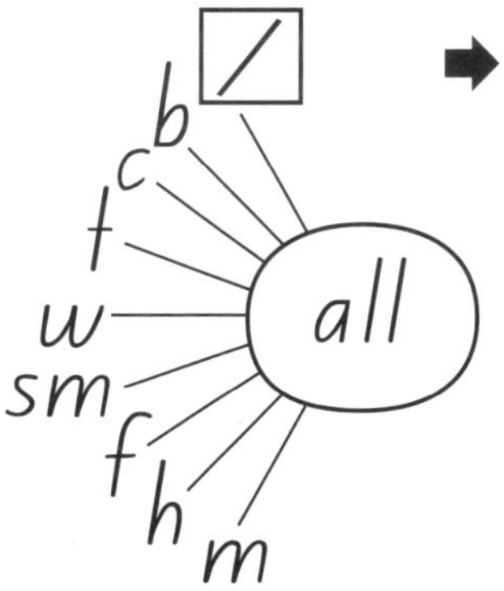

all

12.

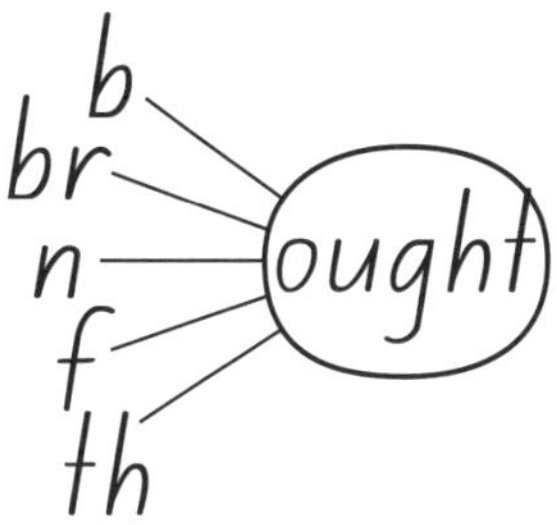

13.

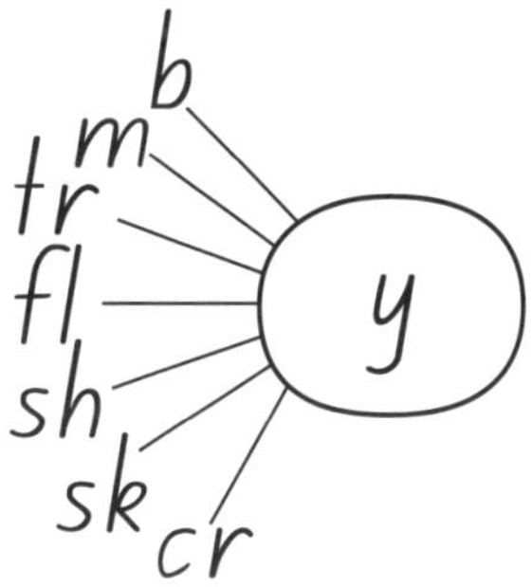

14.

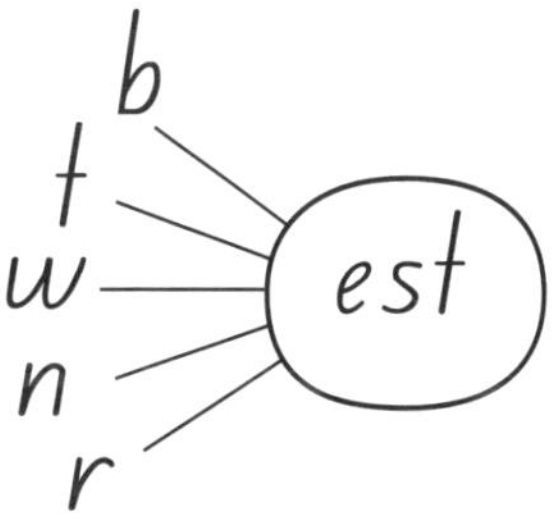

15.

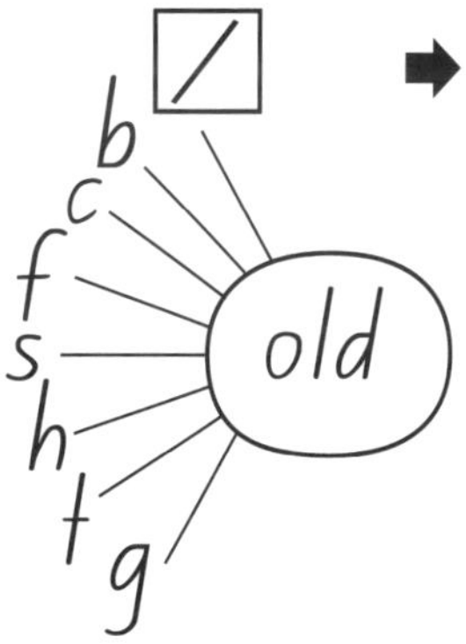

16.

Write the Words (1)

Write these words – from the last 2 pages – under the pictures.

look	cat	sad	see	play	men
three	ten	day	dad	light	book
say	bat	night	mat	mad	cook
fight	hot	pen	took	sat	tree

s

3

m

(past)
t

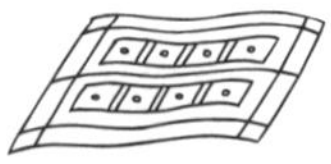
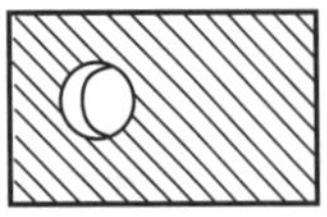

l
10

(past)

Write the Words (2)

Continue writing the words.

star	ball	wake	west	car	ring
shy	cold	sing	nought	spring	fly
fought	wing	take	told	cake	sky
lake	hat	cry	rat	thought	

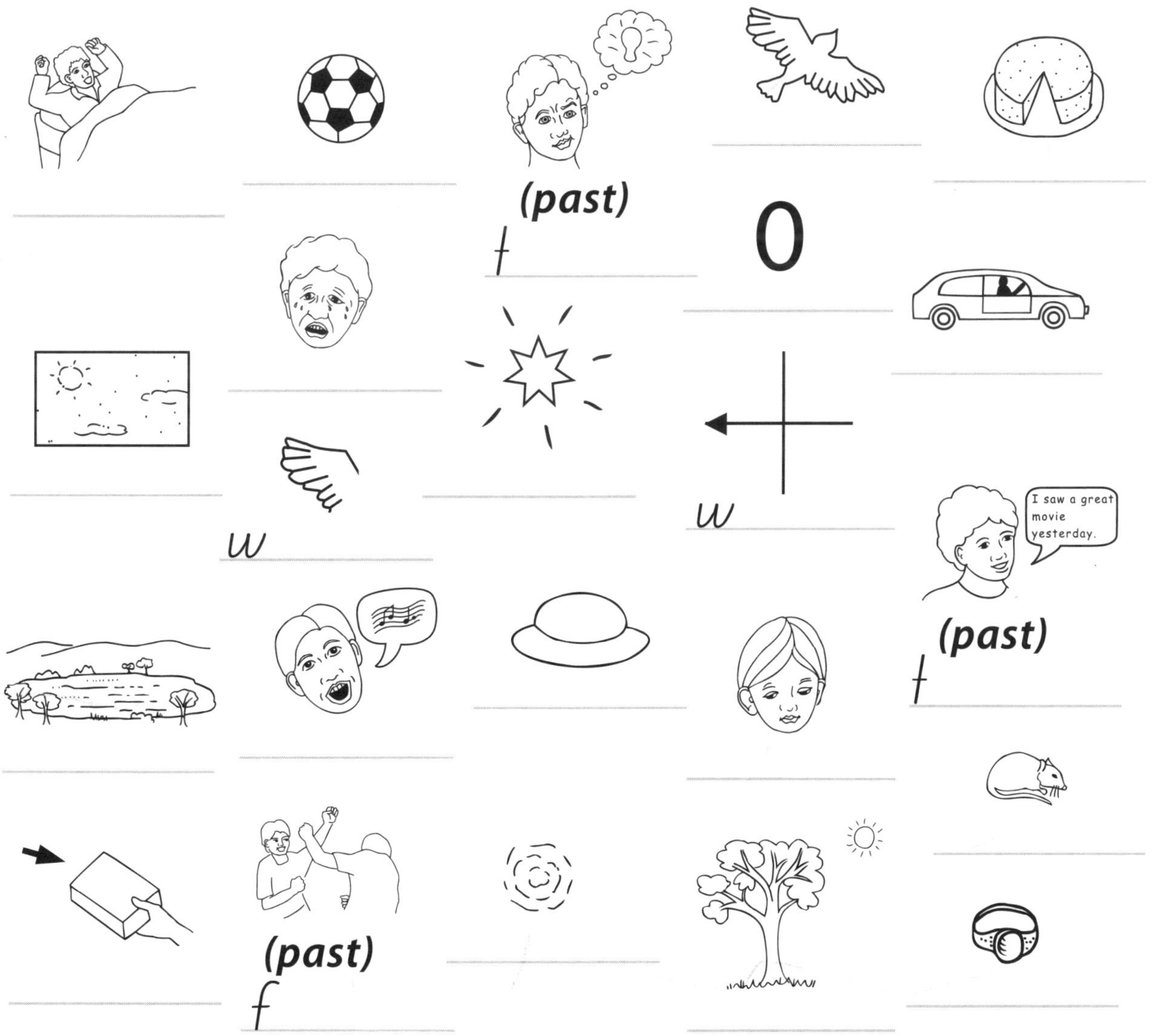

Making Sentences (1)

Write the missing letters – from the last 4 pages – in the words below to make the sentences.

1. It is not _ot . (h – n)
2. _ook  in the _oo**d** _ook_ook .
   (g – L – b – c)
3. She can _ee  _ _ _ee [3] _ _ee**n**
   _ _ee**s** . (thr – tr – gr – s)
4. That was my _est _est. (t – b)
5. The _at _at  _at on the _at 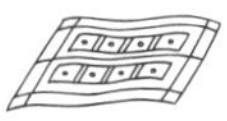.
   (f – s – c – m)
6. They _ay _ _ay  to_ay. (pl – m – d)
7. We can _ake a _ake . (c – m)
8. _ _en there were _en [10] _en .
   (t – Th – m)

Making Sentences (2)

Continue writing the missing letters.

9. She is _all, not __all. (t - sm)

10. I felt _ad , _ad  and _ad, but now I feel __ad. (b - gl - m - s)

11. __ing me the _ing . (r - Br)

12. _y bird will __y to __y  to the __y . (fl - sk - tr - M)

13. I __ought  I __ought it. (th - br)

14. I _ight turn on the __ight _ight  to_ight. (l - n - m - br)

15. The __**ars**  are _ar away. (f - st)

16. He _old me they _old the old car. (t - s)

Can I borrow it? (1)

Write the names of the items.
Also write what one student asks and what the other student answers.
Use full stops, commas and question marks.

➡ Talking and Listening:

Can I borrow it? (2)A

Student A: ASK THE QUESTIONS.

Ask Student B if you can borrow these things.
Write what you ask and write the answers.

YOU ASK. ⬇

Can I borrow your Pencil, please?

______________.

Can I borrow your ruler, Please?

____

____
____
measure
____

____

____
____
____
____

____

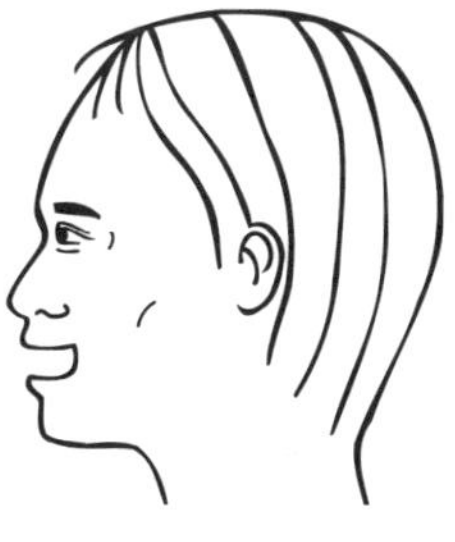

Can I borrow your some peapes Please ?

____

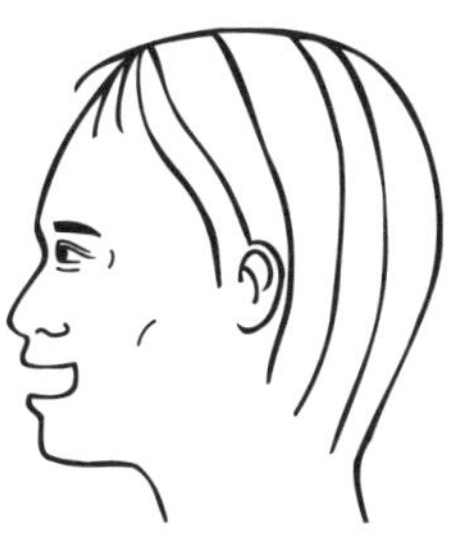

Talking and Listening:

Can I borrow it?(2)B

Student B: ANSWER THE QUESTIONS.

Write what Student A asks you and write what you answer.

Talking and Listening:

Can I borrow it? (3)A

Student A: ANSWER THE QUESTIONS.

Tell your partner if he/ she can borrow these things.
Write the questions and your replies.

YOU ANSWER.

➡ Talking and Listening:

Can I borrow it? (3)B

Student B: ASK THE QUESTIONS.

Ask your partner if you can borrow these things.

Write your questions and the replies.

YOU ASK.

Actions (1)

What are they doing?

What is he/ she doing?

Write the simple verbs under the pictures.

➡ 1. talk

2. ________

3. ________

4. ________

5. ________

6. ________

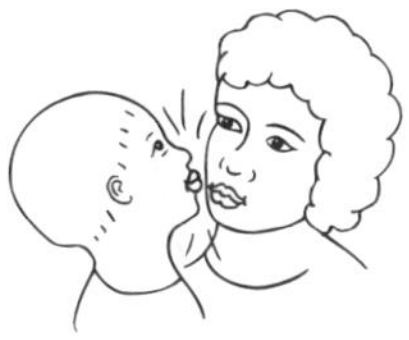

7. ________

8. ________

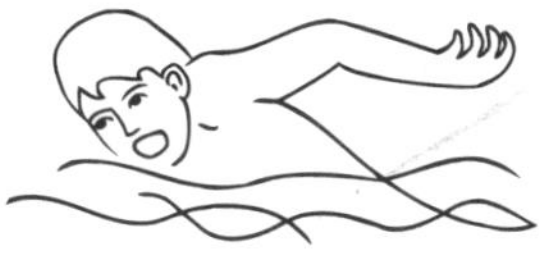

9. ________

10. ________

11. ________

12. draw

13. ________

14. ________

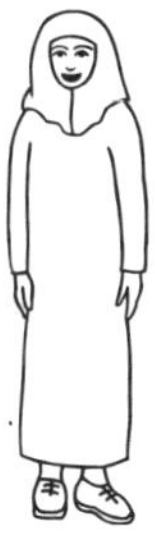

15. ________

16. ch

Actions (2)

What are they doing?

What is she/ he doing?

Join the parts of the sentences (using the present continuous verbs: with -ing).

Copy the sentences underneath.

1.	The boy	is writing.
2.	The girl	is listening.
3.	The man	is looking.
4.	The woman	is reading.
5.	The boy	is talking.
6.	The girl	are kissing.
7.	The boy	is walking.
8.	The woman and baby	is singing.

1. The boy is reading
2. The girl is
3. The man is writing
4. The woman is Talking
5. The boy is singing
6. The girl is
7. The boy is listening
8. The woman and baby are Kissing

Actions (3)

What are they doing?

What is he/ she doing?

Continue writing the sentences.

9.	The boy	is sitting.
10.	The woman	is swimming.
11.	The man	is standing.
12.	The girl	is drawing.
13.	The boy	is typing.
14.	The girl	are dancing.
15.	The people	is running.
16.	The girl and boy	are chatting.

9. The boy is Swimming

10. The woman is

11. The man is sitting

12. The girl is

13. The boy drawing

14. The girl

15. The people are dancing

16. The girl and boy chatting.

Making Words (3)

2-Syllable Words A

Join the syllables to make the correct words.
Write the words under the pictures.

1.	bed	coat
2.	net	brush
3.	rain	chair
4.	paint	room
5.	arm	shoes
6.	sport	ball

7.	glas	ther
8.	hap	ping
9.	shop	tion
10.	cir	ses
11.	fa	cle
12.	ques	py

bed room

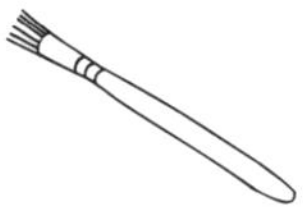

Question

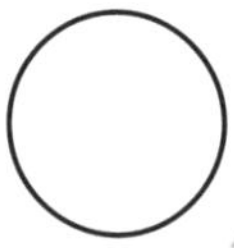
circle

father

shopping

happ

Making Words (4)

2-Syllable Words B

Continue from the last page.

13.	thirs	ny
14.	sun	sic
15.	six	ches
16.	let	ty
17.	mat	ty
18.	mu	ter

19.	pa	ble
20.	T	ple
21.	chic	vie
22.	ta	per
23.	mo	V
24.	ap	ken

60

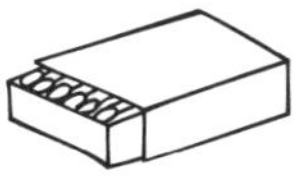

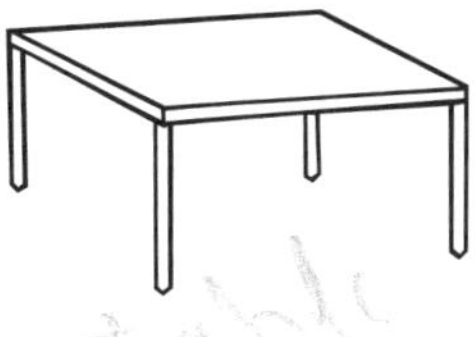

Making Sentences (3)

2-Syllable Words

Now write the missing letters in the words – from the last 2 pages – to complete the sentences.

1. She feels hap__.
2. It's a sun__ day.
3. His __ther told him.
4. Could I have another _____brush?
5. This ___chair is big.
6. Do you like this __sic?
7. That's a good ques____.
8. My ____coat is in the ___room.
9. We went shop____ for new ______shoes.
10. He saw that __vie on T_.
11. Put the __per on the ta___.
12. The chic___ is eating seeds.
13. They'll play net____ on Friday.
14. There are ___ty seconds in one minute.
15. Do you want an app__?

Join the Dots (1)

Make a picture:

First join the numbers.
Then join the letters to make a picture.
What is it?

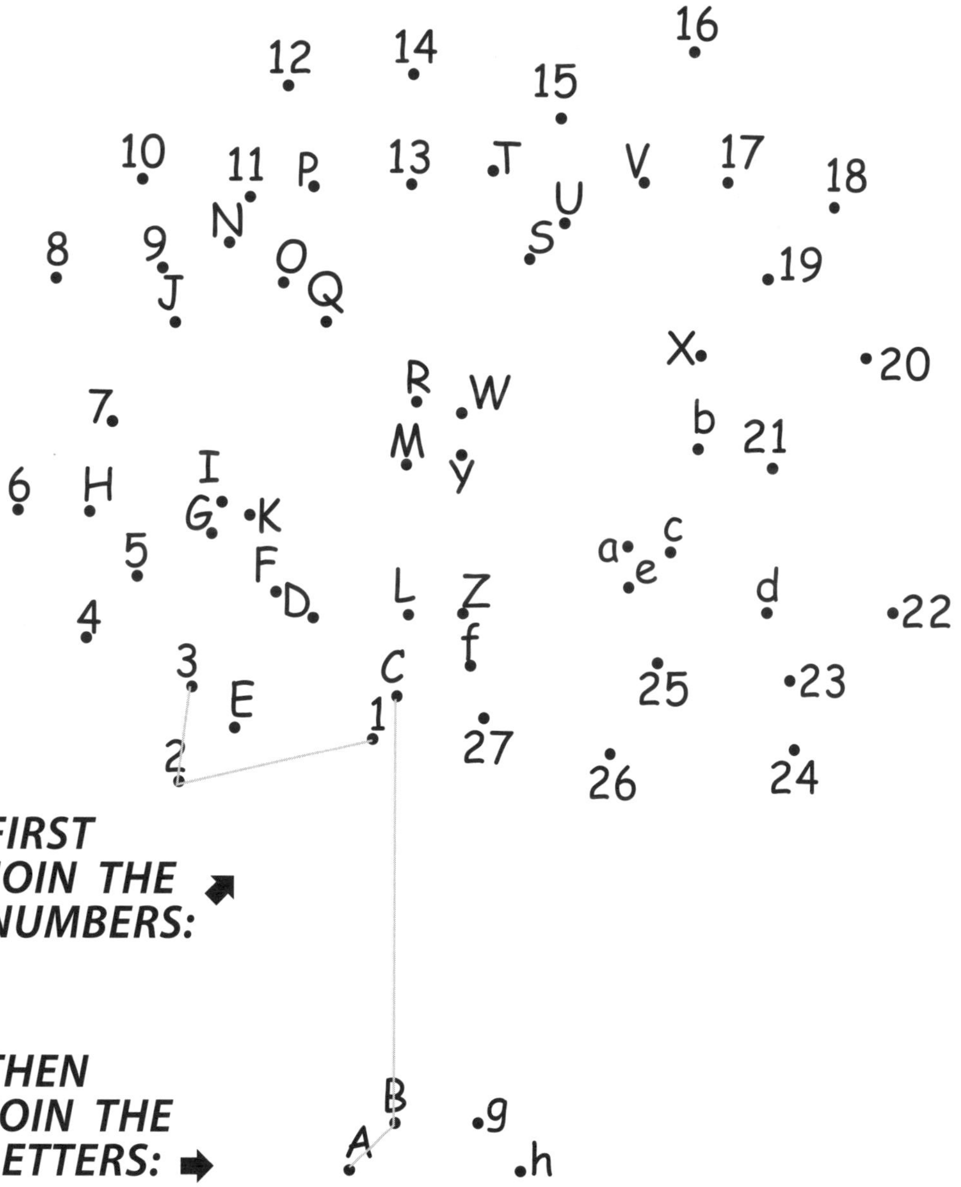

FIRST JOIN THE NUMBERS:

THEN JOIN THE LETTERS:

The picture is a ________________.

Join the Dots (2)

Make a picture:

Now the letters are mixed up. Read how to join the letters to make the picture. What is it?

1. *Join D to G. Then join G to B.*
2. *Join B to E. Then join E to G.*
3. *Join G to V. Then join V to E.*
4. *Join E to P. Then join P to C.*
5. *Join C to T. Then join T to Q.*
6. *Join Q to U. Then join U to W.*
7. *Join W to A. Then join A to K.*
8. *Join K to J. Then join J to Z.*
9. *Join Z to M. Then join M to N.*
10. *Join N to X. Then join X to F.*
11. *Join F to Y. Then join Y to H.*
12. *Lastly, join H to P.*

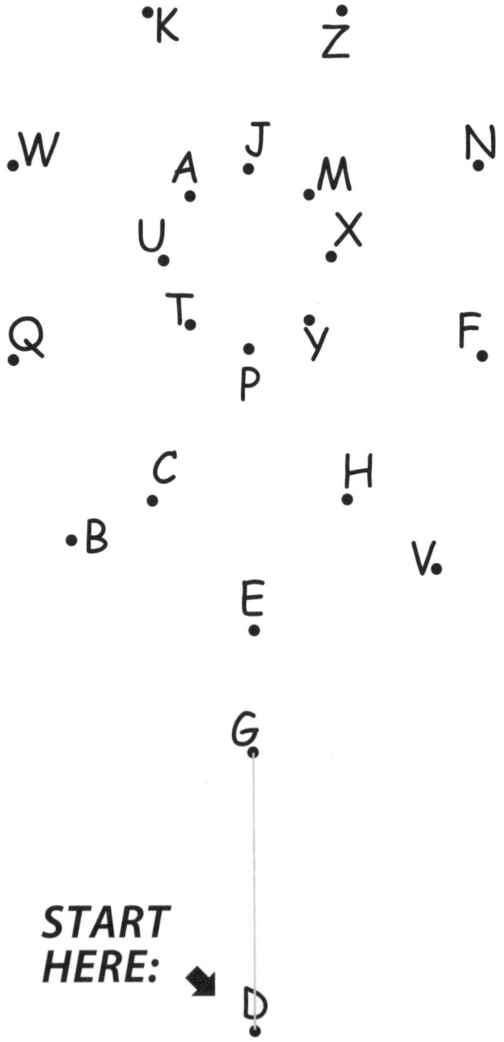

➡ ***The picture is a ______________ .***

➡ Talking and Listening:

Join the Dots (3)A

Student A:

The letters are out of order.
Tell your partner (Student B) which letters to join to make the picture.
Write and join the letters that your partner tells you.

1. *Join A to P. Then join P to C.*
2. *Join ___ to ___. Then join ___ to ___.*
3. *Join D to M. Then join M to Z.*
4. *Join ___ to ___. Then join ___ to ___.*
5. *Join F to N. Then join N to B.*
6. *Join ___ to ___. Then join ___ to ___.*
7. *Join Q to I. Then join I to W.*
8. *Join ___ to ___. Then join ___ to ___.*
9. *Join X to J. Then join J to Y.*
10. *Join ___ to ___. Lastly, join ___ to ___.*

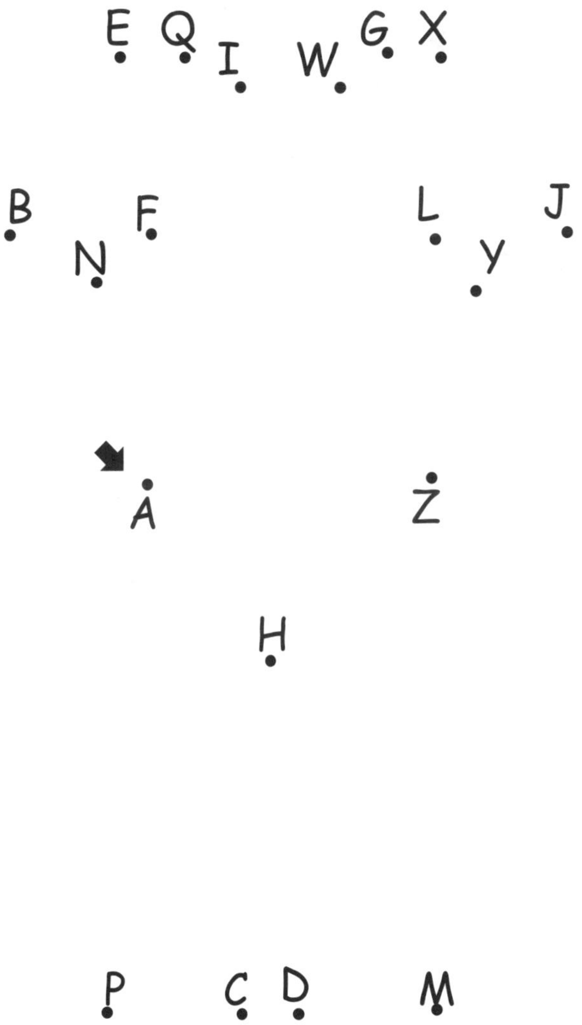

➡ ***The picture is a ______________ and ______________.***

➡ Talking and Listening:

Join the Dots (3)B

Student B:

The letters are out of order.
Tell your partner (Student A) which letters to join to make the picture.
Write and join the letters that your partner tells you.

1. *Join ___ to ___. Then join ___ to ___.*
2. *Join C to H. Then join H to D.*
3. *Join ___ to ___. Then join ___ to ___.*
4. *Join Z to A. Then join A to F.*
5. *Join ___ to ___. Then join ___ to ___.*
6. *Join B to E. Then join E to Q.*
7. *Join ___ to ___. Then join ___ to ___.*
8. *Join W to G. Then join G to X.*
9. *Join ___ to ___. Then join ___ to ___.*
10. *Join Y to L. Lastly, join L to Z.*

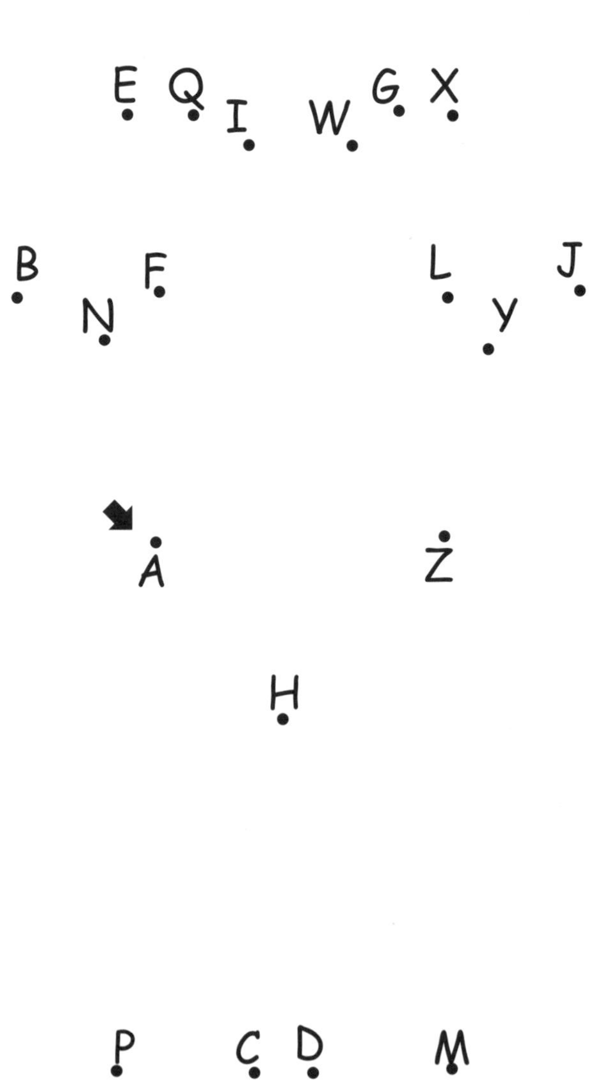

➡ ***The picture is a ______________ and ______________.***

Choose the Word (2)

Put a circle around the correct word in each row.

1.		word	world	wall	work
2.		heart	aunt	art	hard
3.		threw	those	through	throw
4.		cut	coat	kick	truck
5.	8	ate	eight	eighty	eighteen
6.		shape	street	sheep	sleep
7.		thin	thing	thank	think
8.		scissors	soccer	circle	sentence
9.		shop	sheep	ship	dish
10.		catch	cash	check	such

Places (1)

What are these places?

What is this place?

Write the name of each place under the picture.

12. ____________

____

7. ____________

13. ____________

5. across ____________

10. ____________

____

1. ____________

6. ____________

2. ____________

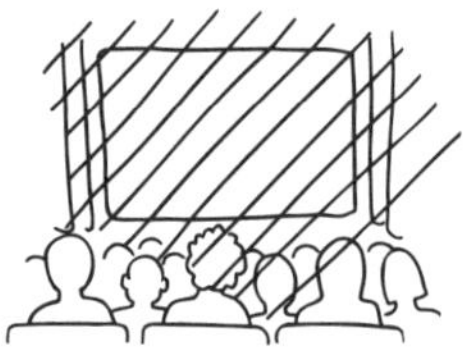

8. ____________

3. ____________

____

11. ____________

5. down ____________

____

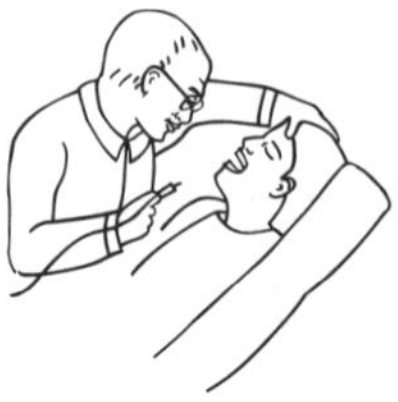

9. ____________

4. ____________

14. ____________

Places (2)

Crossword Puzzle

Write the words onto the crossword puzzle.
They go ACROSS ➡ and DOWN ⬇.

Places (3)

What do people do there?

Write the names of the places – from the last 2 pages – in the sentences.

1. People catch a bus at the ________ ________.
2. People catch the train at the ________ ________.
3. Students study at ________.
4. People watch a movie at the ________.
5. People get their money at the ________.
6. People send letters at the ________ ________.
7. People walk, sit and play at the ________.
8. People get their teeth fixed at the ________.
9. People read books at the ________.
10. People go swimming at the ________ ________.
11. People look at animals at the ________.
12. Sick people get help at the ________.
13. People buy and sell things at the ________.
14. There are many buildings and people in the ________.
15. There are some trees and not many people in the ________.

➡ Talking and Listening: 

Conversation 1(A)

Student A:

Read this conversation with your partner and write the missing words.

➡

➡ Talking and Listening: 

Conversation 1(B)

Student B:

Read this conversation with your partner and write the missing words.

➡ Talking and Listening:

Alphabetical Order(1)A

Student A:

Copy these words in alphabetical order.
Then read the words to your partner.
Write your missing words.

on	cards	under	yesterday
smile	my	internet	window
keep	and	eat	quick
give			

➡ a	and	j		s	
b		k		t	
c		l		u	
d		m		v	
e		n		w	
f		o		x	
g		p		y	
h		q		z	
i		r			

➡ Talking and Listening:

Alphabetical Order(1)B

Student B:

Copy these words in alphabetical order.
Then read the words to your partner.
Write your missing words.

twenty help zigzag x-ray	put no line	jump remember book	date forget very

a		j		s	
b	book	k		t	
c		l		u	
d		m		v	
e		n		w	
f		o		x	
g		p		y	
h		q		z	
i		r			

Feelings (1)

How do they feel?

How does she/ he feel?

Write sentences. Continue on the next page.

▸ **He / She** (He circled) **feels** thoughtful.

hot thoughtful relaxed	tired shy bored	hungry angry thirsty

1.  He feels ____________________

2. 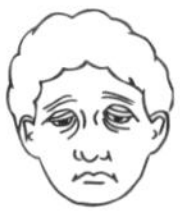 ____________________

3.  ____________________

4.  ____________________

5. 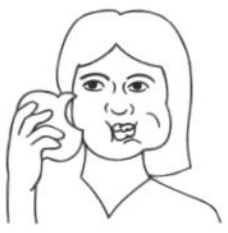 ____________________

6.  ____________________

7.  ____________________

8.  ____________________

9.  ____________________

Feelings (2)

How do they feel?

Continue making the sentences.

cold sick happy	sad confused excited	scared surprised worried

10.  happy

11.  Surprised

12.  excited

13.  worried scared

14.  Sad

15.  confused

16.  woried

17.  sick

18.  cold

Feelings (3)

Word Search

Find the feeling adjectives on the word search.
They go ACROSS ➡ and DOWN ⬇.

T	H	O	U	G	H	T	F	U	L	Q	Z	S	I	C	K
S	A	D	G	S	O	Q	B	B	B	H	G	H	C	Q	K
U	F	J	Y	T	K	Q	C	K	H	O	U	Y	L	N	M
R	L	E	T	R	X	V	W	L	I	T	U	C	O	L	D
P	Z	X	P	Q	R	A	K	K	Y	T	F	C	O	O	Q
R	U	C	L	G	S	U	F	L	I	G	J	H	P	F	P
I	G	I	H	V	L	Z	C	N	W	O	R	R	I	E	D
S	P	T	A	X	P	X	O	A	R	E	L	A	X	E	D
E	F	E	P	Q	E	I	C	O	N	F	U	S	E	D	E
D	K	D	P	A	D	L	S	C	A	R	E	D	N	A	S
W	Z	J	Y	H	U	F	F	L	M	I	Z	F	T	J	B
R	E	Q	Z	E	E	A	P	L	M	M	P	O	U	Q	P
X	G	I	O	O	O	P	S	S	D	H	U	N	G	R	Y
P	L	K	A	N	G	R	Y	B	O	R	E	D	P	Y	D
T	H	I	R	S	T	Y	O	Q	T	I	R	E	D	O	V
I	E	G	Y	U	U	G	H	N	M	K	Y	E	E	A	O

➡ ***How do you feel?***
I feel ________________.

Find a Word (1)

Look in 'Spark! Wordbank' and find the topics.
Write the page numbers and topics.
Then find examples.

▶ *Find* ***a / an*** *place ____* ***that*** ***starts / begins*** ***with*** *s.*

1. ***TOPIC: <u>Places</u>: page numbers:*** 6–9 ____

*(a) Find a place ____ that starts with s. **EXAMPLE:** shop ____*

(b) Find a place ____ that begins with h. ____

(c) Find a ____ that begins with l. ____

---

2. ***TOPIC: <u>Sport</u>: page number:*** ____

*(a) Find a sport ____ that starts with t. **EXAMPLE:** ____*

(b) Find a ____ that begins with f. ____

(c) Find a ____ that begins with b. ____

---

3. ***<u>Feelings</u>: page numbers:*** ____

(a) Find a feeling ____ that starts with h. ____

(b) Find another ____ that ____ with h. ____

(c) Find a ____ that ____ with a. ____

---

4. ***<u>Animals</u>: page numbers:*** ____

(a) Find an animal ____ that begins with k. ____

(b) Find another ____ that ____ with k. ____

(c) Find an ____ that ____ with d. ____

---

5. ***<u>Colours</u>: page number:*** ____ ***YOU CHOOSE:***

(a) Find a colour ____ that ____ with ___. ____

(b) Find a ____ that ____ with ___. ____

(c) Find a ____ that ____ with ___. ____

➡ Talking and Listening: 

Find a Word (2)A

Student A:

Tell your partner:

▶ ***Find a / an ________ that starts / begins with __ .***

Write the numbers, topics, letters and examples.

1. Places: page numbers: 6 – 9
(a) Find a place ________ that begins with z. ________
(b) Find a ________ that starts with __ . ________
(c) Find a ________ that begins with b. ________

2. Sport: page number: ________
(a) Find a sport ________ that starts with __ . ________
(b) Find a ________ that begins with s. ________
(c) Find a ________ that begins with __ . ________

3. Feelings: page numbers: ________
(a) Find a feeling ________ that begins with s. ________
(b) Find another ________ that ________ with __ . ________
(c) Find a ________ that ________ with t. ________

4. Animals: page numbers: ________ **YOU CHOOSE:**
(a) Find an animal ________ that ________ with __ . ________
(b) Find an ________ that ________ with __ . ________
(c) Find an ________ that ________ with __ . ________

5. Colours: page number: ________
(a) Find a colour ________ that ________ with __ . ________
(b) Find a ________ that ________ with __ . ________
(c) Find a ________ that ________ with __ . ________

Find a Word (2)B

Student B:

Tell your partner:

▶ ***Find*** **a / an** ______ ***that*** **starts / begins** ***with*** __ .

Write the numbers, topics, letters and examples.

1. Places: page numbers: 6 – 9

(a) Find a place ______ that begins with __ . ______

(b) Find a ______ that starts with d . ______

(c) Find a ______ that begins with __ . ______

2. Sport: page number: ______

(a) Find a sport ______ that starts with v . ______

(b) Find a ______ that begins with __ . ______

(c) Find a ______ that begins with c . ______

3. Feelings: page numbers: ______

(a) Find a feeling ______ that begins with __ . ______

(b) Find another ______ that ______ with s . ______

(c) Find a ______ that ______ with __ . ______

4. Animals: page numbers: ______ **YOU CHOOSE:**

(a) Find an animal ______ that ______ with __ . ______

(b) Find an ______ that ______ with __ . ______

(c) Find an ______ that ______ with __ . ______

5. Colours: page number: ______

(a) Find a colour ______ that ______ with __ . ______

(b) Find a ______ that ______ with __ . ______

(c) Find a ______ that ______ with __ . ______

➡ Talking and Listening:

Letters (1)A

Vowels (Student A):

Read the capital letter vowels to your partner.
Write the vowels your partner reads to you.
Then write them in small letters.

➡ 1. A a	3. I	5. U
➡ 2.	4.	6. [ ]

Consonants (Student A):

Now read and write the capital letter consonants and write them in small letters.

➡ 1. B	8.	15. S
➡ 2.	9. L	16.
3. D	10.	17. V
4.	11. N	18.
5. G	12.	19. X
6.	13. Q	20.
7. J	14.	21. Z

➡ Talking and Listening:

Letters (1)B

Vowels (Student B):

Read the capital letter vowels to your partner.
Write the vowels your partner reads to you.
Then write them in small letters.

➡	1.	3.	5.
➡	2. E e	4. O	6. [Y]

Consonants (Student B):

Now read and write the capital letter consonants
and write them in small letters.

➡	1.	8. K	15.
➡	2. C	9.	16. T
	3.	10. M	17.
	4. F	11.	18. W
	5.	12. P	19.
	6. H	13.	20. Y
	7.	14. R	21.

Choose the Word (3)

Put a circle around the correct word in each row.

1.		*square*	*where*	*went*	*west*
2.	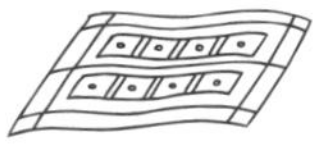	*met*	*mat*	*time*	*mad*
3.		*right*	*late*	*light*	*let*
4.		*dear*	*lead*	*read*	*red*
5.		*nose*	*snow*	*note*	*no*
6.		*fun*	*knife*	*fine*	*phone*
7.	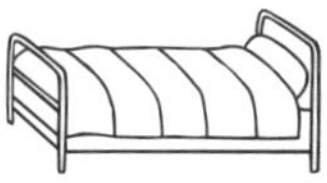	*bad*	*dad*	*bed*	*bread*
8.		*said*	*sad*	*sat*	*side*
9.		*east*	*seat*	*eat*	*tea*
10.		*air*	*rain*	*ran*	*near*

Different Sounds (1)

Vowels: short

Write the missing short vowel sounds in these words.

c_t t_xi c_mel v_n b_dminton k_ngaroo

t_nnis f_rry _lephant n_tball

cr_cket sh_p f_sh ch_cken tax_ badm_nton

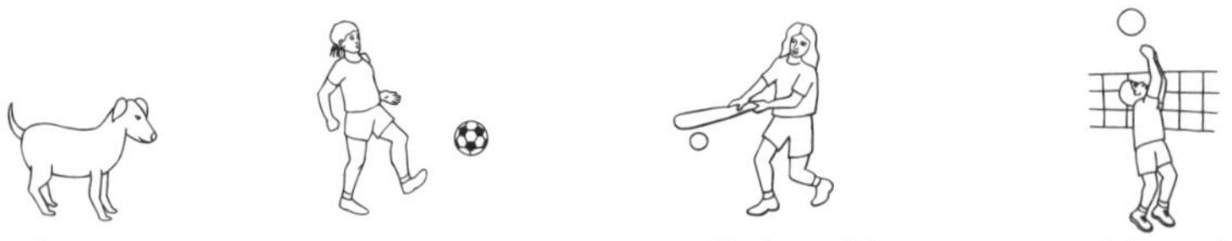

d_g s_ccer s_ftball v_lleyball

tr_ck k_ng fu d_ck r_gby b_s b_ffalo

Grouping Words (1)

Vowels: short

Now write the words in the correct groups.
Just write each word once.

Sports	Animals	Transport

1. *Badminton is a* sport .
2. *A camel is an* Animals .
3. *An elephant is an* Animals .
4. *A van is a type of* Transport .

Different Sounds (2)

Vowels: long

Write the missing long vowel sounds in these words. (You might need to check the spellings.)

➡ c_k_ r_ _ncoat l_k_ _TM r_ _lway st_tion

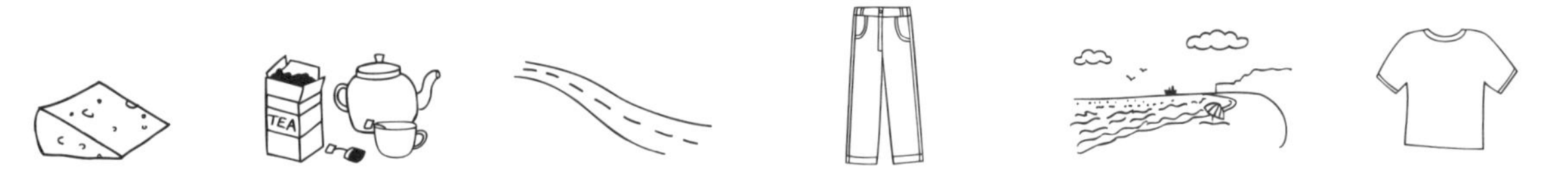

ch_ _se t_ _ str_ _t j_ _ns b_ _ch t_ _shirt

l_brary r_c_ l_ghts _cecream t_ _ p_neapple

tomat_ c_ _t potat_ h_m_ r_ _d p_st office

m_vies fr_ _t z_ _ s_ _p swims_ _t n_ _dles

h_ _se caulifl_ _er t_ _n tr_ _sers

pyj_mas p_ _k g_ _lic sc_ _f f_ _m c_ _digan

Grouping Words (2)

Vowels: long

Now write the words in the correct groups.

Places	*Foods*	*Clothes*

1. *A street is a* places ______ .
2. *A tomato is a* foods ______ .
3. *Cheese is a* ______ .
4. *A raincoat is a type of* ______ .
5. *Jeans are a type of* clothes ______ .

Colours (1)

What are these colours?

What is this colour? Colour the squares.

red	pink
yellow	light blue
blue	light green
orange	dark blue
green	dark green
purple	brown
	black
	white
	grey

Colour this pattern.

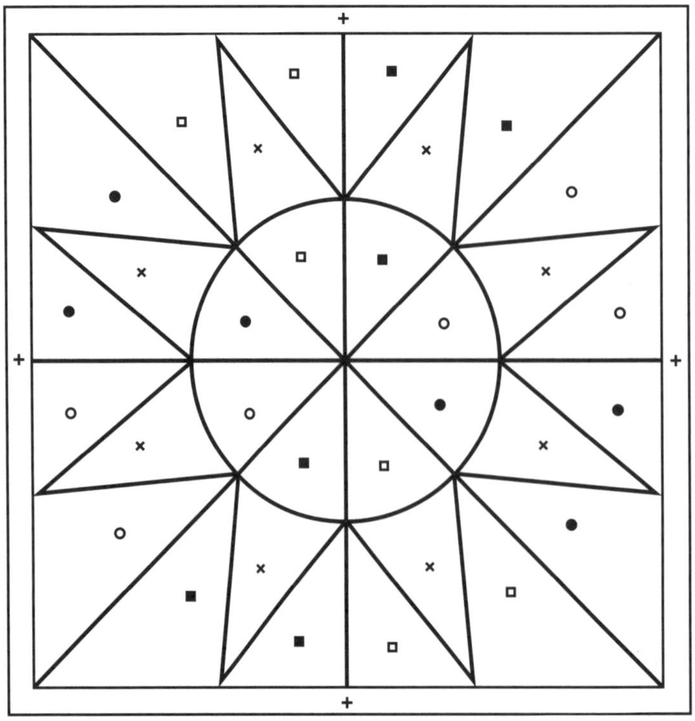

red □
orange ■
yellow ○
green ×
blue +
purple •

Colours (2)

Word Search

Find the names of the colours on the word search.
They go ACROSS ➡ and DOWN ⬇.
After you find them, write them underneath.

Y	E	L	L	O	W	I	P	X	L	D	F	J	L	S	E
L	M	K	R	G	R	E	Y	Q	I	A	P	U	D	F	R
I	G	J	K	S	C	M	A	E	G	R	E	D	K	S	E
Z	S	R	L	J	C	V	S	Q	H	K	S	L	E	D	X
U	Q	E	K	O	Z	A	I	I	T	G	L	N	P	F	B
K	E	P	B	B	R	O	W	N	B	R	M	Q	L	P	H
O	Y	S	L	F	K	E	W	P	L	E	D	L	J	O	J
P	B	J	D	A	R	K	B	L	U	E	F	I	V	W	O
I	L	S	G	R	E	E	N	M	E	N	N	G	N	Y	W
Z	A	A	C	W	J	S	A	K	D	V	A	H	L	E	I
J	C	K	A	A	Z	H	E	O	W	H	I	T	E	I	U
Y	K	U	W	L	H	B	J	P	I	N	K	G	M	U	H
P	U	C	P	L	G	P	V	N	Z	H	U	R	N	U	B
Y	R	M	S	A	J	X	O	R	A	N	G	E	F	N	L
I	L	S	C	X	K	X	P	U	R	P	L	E	O	T	U
I	D	G	I	T	Y	R	P	Q	Q	B	K	N	P	D	E

Colour & Shape (1)

What are these shapes?

What is this shape? Colour each 2D shape. Choose your own colours.

Then make sentences about each shape.

▶ ***This is a / an*** purple circle.

circle	***rectangle***	***star***
diamond	***square***	***ellipse***
triangle	***heart***	***polygon***

➡ ***1.*** 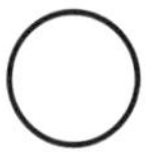 This is a circle

2. 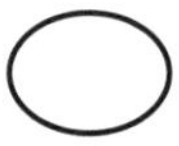 This is a ellipse

3.  This is a square

4. 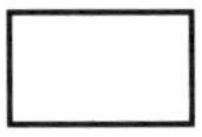 this is a regtangle

5.  This is a triangle

6.  This is a polygon

7.  This is a diamond

8.  This is a star

9.  This is a heart

➡ Talking and Listening:

Colour & Shape (2)A

Student A:

Tell your partner how to draw and colour the shapes.
Draw and colour your shapes inside the boxes.
Then write sentences describing the shapes.

- ***This is a*** red polygon .
- ***These are*** yellow stars .

1. *Draw a polygon.*
   Colour it red.
   This is a ________________

2. *Draw a* ________ .
   Colour it ________ .
   ____

3. *Draw 3 circles.*
   Colour them orange.
   These are ________________

4. ________________
   ____
   ____

5. *Draw 4 squares.*
   Colour them black.
   ____

6. ________________
   ____
   ____

➡ Talking and Listening:

Colour & Shape (2)B

Student B:

Tell your partner how to draw and colour the shapes.
Draw and colour your shapes inside the boxes.
Then write sentences describing the shapes.

- ***This is a*** red polygon .
- ***These are*** yellow stars .

1. Draw a ________ .
   Colour it ________ .
   This is a ________

2. Draw a triangle.
   Colour it blue.
   ____

3. ________
   ____
   These are ________

4. Draw 3 stars.
   Colour them yellow.
   ____

5. ________
   ____
   ____

6. Draw 5 hearts.
   Colour them pink.
   ____

Maths

What are the answers?

What is the answer?

First write the answers in numbers underneath.

Then write them in words on the crossword puzzle.

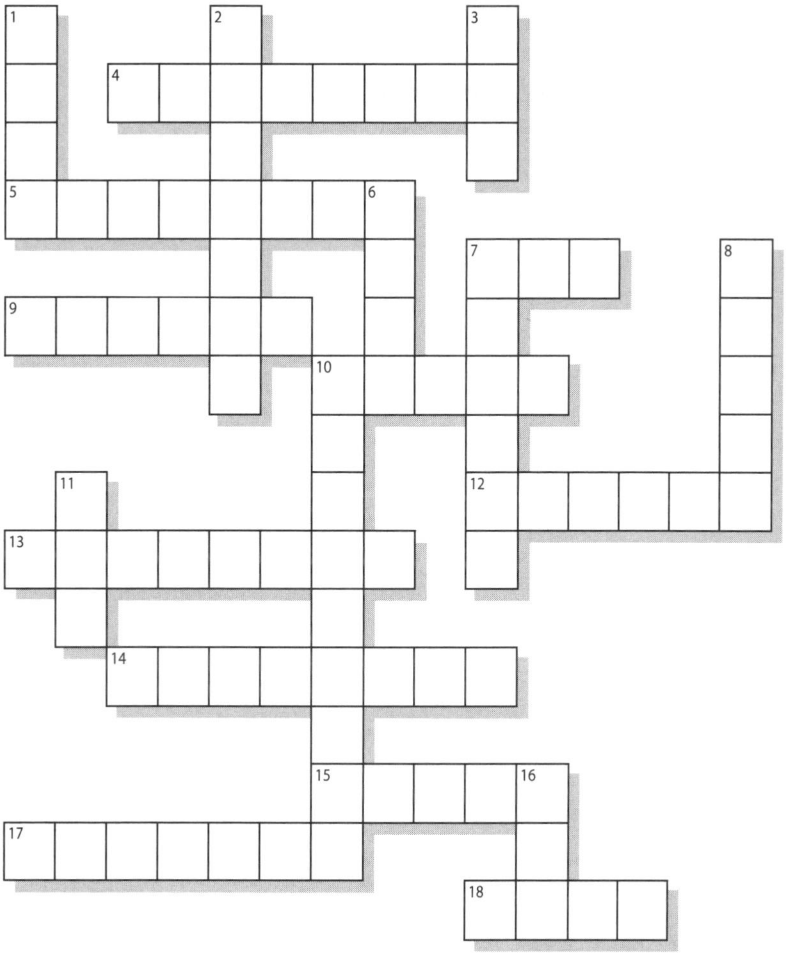

1.	$3 + 2 =$	**10. across**	$4 + 3 =$
2.	$10 + 6 =$	**10. down**	$4 + 13 =$
3.	$12 - 11 =$	**11.**	$9 - 3 =$
4.	$15 - 2 =$	**12.**	$10 + 2 =$
5.	$9 + 9 =$	**13.**	$20 - 1 =$
6.	$10 - 1 =$	**14.**	$4 + 10 =$
7. across	$5 + 5 =$	**15.**	$4 + 4 =$
7. down	$11 + 9 =$	**16.**	$10 - 8 =$
8.	$6 - 3 =$	**17.**	$20 - 5 =$
9.	$9 + 2 =$	**18.**	$10 - 6 =$

A School Day (1)

Write the missing words about Anna's school day.

(1) Before School

1. *In the morning before school, I usually* 

→ *get up* *at 6.30.*

2. *Then I*  have shower *or* 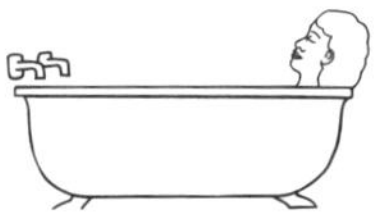

bath *.*

3. *I*  dress *and* 

do my hear *at 7 o'clock.*

4. *At 7.10 I*  have breakfast *and* 

drink coffee *.*

5. *After that, I*  brush *.*

6. *I* 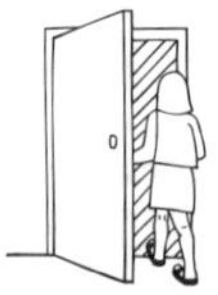 leave *at 7.30.*

A School Day (2)

Continue writing the missing words in the story.

(2) At School

1. *At 7.45, I catch the* 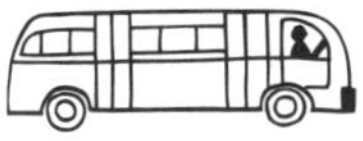 bus *to*

 school*. I get there at 8.15.*

2. *School starts at 8.45.*

3. *We do many things at school. We work and study and also play.*

4. *We*  think, 

Talk,

 listen,  ask, 

answer,

 read,  write, 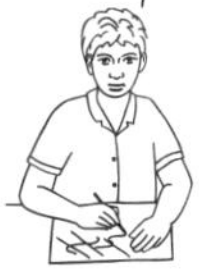 draw,

 computing*, etc.*

5. *School finishes at 3.10.*

A School Day (3)

Continue writing the missing words in the recount.

(3) After School

1. I usually  get home at 4.00.

2. Then I might  watch TV or  listen to music.

3. At 5.30 I might  Reed on night.

4. I  have dinner at 7 o'clock and  wash the diches.

5. I usually  go to bed at 8 o'clock, or sometimes 9.30.

A School Day (4)

What time does it happen?

Now fill in the times in the boxes.

TIMES	ACTIVITIES
➡ 6.30	get up
	get dressed
	have breakfast
	leave home
	catch the bus to school
	get to school
	school starts
	school finishes
	get home
	do my homework
	have dinner and wash the dishes
	go to bed

➡ Talking and Listening:

Your School Day

Ask one of your classmates about their school day.

- ***What time do you*** get up ***?***
- ***What time does*** school start ***?***

	ACTIVITIES	TIMES
➡ 1.	*What time do you get up?*	
2.	*What time do you have breakfast?*	
3.	*What time do you leave your home?*	
4.	*What time do you get to school?*	
5.	*What time does school start?*	
6.	*What time does school finish?*	
7.	*What time do you get home?*	
8.	*What time do you do your homework?*	
9.	*What time do you have dinner?*	
10.	*What time do you go to bed?*	

My School Day

Write about your own school day.

- *I* get up *at* 7.00 *.*
- *Then I* ________________ *.*
- *After that, I* ________________ *at* ________ *.*
- *At* ________ *I* ________________ *.*

(1) Before School

➡

(2) At School

(3) After School

Vowels: Short (1)

▶ a

cat

man

▶ e

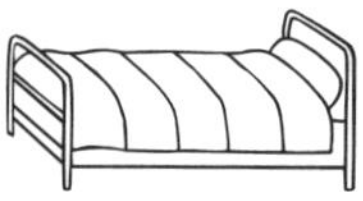
bed

bread

friends

▶ i – y

fish

gym

women

ALSO:
* build

▶ o

dog

watch

cold

ALSO:
* cough

▶ u

sun

monkey

1
one

ALSO:
* flood
* tough

Vowels: Short (2)

▶ oo

book

bush

woman

ALSO:
* should

▶ [ə] ▸ a – e – i – o – u

elephant

table tennis

coloured pencils

biscuits

▶ [ə]

?

question

woman

women

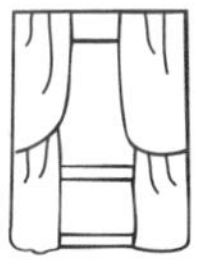

curtain

badminton

▶ [ə]

scissors

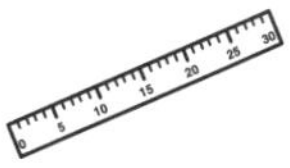

ruler

picture

sandals

painted

ALSO:
* Venus

Vowels: Long (1)

▶ a – ai – ay

baby

rain

play a game

ALSO:
* reins

▶ ee – ea

sheep

tea

key

me

people

ALSO:
* piece
* ceiling
* these

▶ i – y – eye

eye

cry

5
five

light

tie

ALSO:
* hi
* bye
* by
* buy

▶ o – oa – ow

photo

phone

goat

throw

ALSO:
* oh
* though

▶ u – you

unit

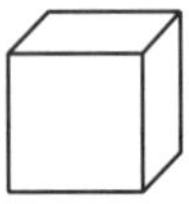
cube

newspaper

computer

ALSO:
* you
* Tuesday
* beautiful

Vowels: Long (2)

▶ oo – u

zoo

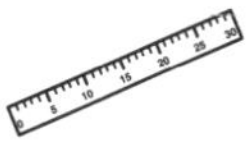
ruler

fruit

soup

glue

shoe

2
two

ALSO:
* **to**
* **too**
* **through**
* **threw**

▶ ir – er – ur

girl

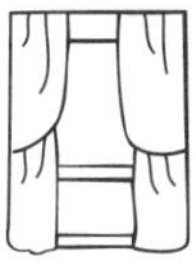
curtain

world

earth

ALSO:
* **her**

▶ or

horse

draw

walk

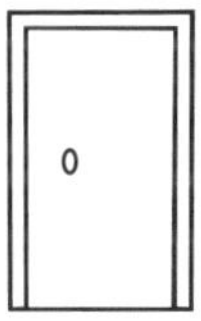
door

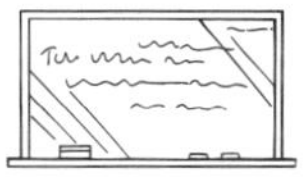
board

4
four

warm

ALSO:
* **because**
* **thought**
* **caught**
* **for**

▶ ar – a

star

heart

ALSO:
* **can't**
* **are**
* **laugh**

Vowels: Long (3)

▶ air

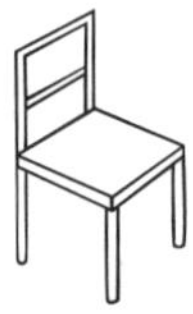
chair

square

ALSO:
* pear
* there
* their
* they're

▶ ear

ear

ALSO:
* hear
* here
* steer

▶ ow – ou

cow

mouse

ALSO:
* drought

▶ oy – oi

boy

oil

Consonants (1)

▶ b

ball

rubbish

▶ c – k

cake

duck

?
question

▶ ch

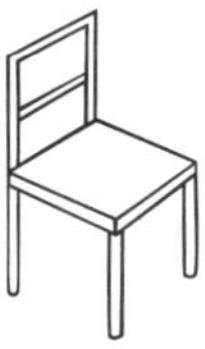
chair

watch

?
question

▶ d

dog

buddha

listened

▶ f

fish

buffalo

phone

▶ g

girl

egg

garbage

▶ h

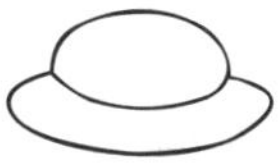
hat

▶ j

jacket

vegetables

garbage

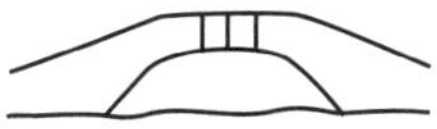
bridge

Consonants (2)

▶ l

lemon

ball

▶ m

man

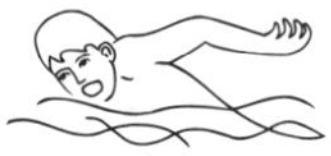
swimming

comb

▶ n

nose

tennis

ALSO:
* know

▶ ng

sing

kangaroo

sink

▶ p

paper

happy

▶ qu (kw)

?
question

▶ r

read

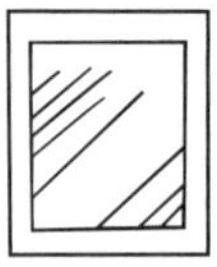
mirror

write

▶ si – s

÷
division

measure

▶ s

soccer

city

scissors

kiss

house

rice

Consonants (3)

▶ sh

sheep

station

ALSO:
* machine
* musician
* sure

▶ t

table

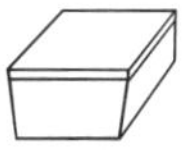
butter

jumped

▶ th (1)

3
three

▶ th (2)

mother

▶ v

vegetables

ALSO:
* have

▶ w

water

wheel

?
question

▶ x (ks)

taxi

ALSO:
* accident
* excellent
* excuse

▶ y

yard

onion

▶ z

zoo

breeze

scissors

ALSO:
* buzz
* busy

Student Record of Achievement:

Name: ______________________

I have completed the work for the following topics:

- ☐ Choose the Word 1,2,3
- ☐ Alphabet
- ☐ Same Letters
- ☐ Same Words 1,2
- ☐ What are they? 1,2
- ☐ Numbers
- ☐ Hi!
- ☐ How many?
- ☐ Alphabet Puzzle
- ☐ Sport
- ☐ Making Words 1-4
- ☐ Write the Words
- ☐ Making Sentences 1-3
- ☐ Can I borrow it?
- ☐ Actions
- ☐ Join the dots
- ☐ Places
- ☐ Conversation
- ☐ Alphabetical Order
- ☐ Feelings
- ☐ Find a Word
- ☐ Letters
- ☐ Different Sounds 1,2
- ☐ Grouping Words 1,2
- ☐ Colour and Shape
- ☐ Maths
- ☐ A School Day

Date completed: ______________